DANCING
with the
UNIVERSE

NINE DIMENSIONS OF LOVE

A *Love Letters From Your Higher Self* Workbook

*Love me when I least deserve it,
because that's when I really need it.*
—SWEDISH PROVERB

DANCING
with the
UNIVERSE

NINE DIMENSIONS OF LOVE

A *Love Letters From Your Higher Self* Workbook

Peri Coeurtney Enkin

CREATORS CHOICE™
Kailua Kona, HI

Dare to Love

–Now is the Time–

Now is the time to know
That all that you do is sacred.
Now, why not consider
A lasting truce with yourself and God?
Now is the time to understand
That all your ideas of right and wrong
Were just a child's training wheels
To be laid aside
When you can finally live
with veracity and love...
Now is the time for the world to know
That every thought and action is sacred.
That this is the time
For you to compute the impossibility
That there is anything
But Grace.
Now is the season to know
That everything you do
Is sacred.

—HAFIZ

Contents

Introduction

LOVE IS INFINITE AND IMPOSSIBLE TO CONTAIN in words or prose. Artists do their best to capture a drop of love's essence and offer it to us through their dance, poetry and painting. These sweet tastes of love's artistry soothe our parched human hearts as water from an oasis quenches our thirst. We need love to survive and thrive. We need love even more to live happy fulfilled lives and to move from mediocrity to excellence.

We spend the majority of our lives waiting for and hoping to hear words of love from others. We wait. We ache. We go without. Love expressed and shared is Magnificent. Living without love and waiting for it to arrive is torture. None of us want to suffer like that and we don't have to. There is no need to starve ourselves or limit our experience of love when we can dare to be both giver and receiver of love right now.

–You Are Invited–

IN *LOVE LETTERS FROM YOUR HIGHER SELF—HOLDING HANDS WITH SPIRIT*, you received thirty-five detailed love letters—each one an outpouring of love for you.

Now, *Dancing with the Universe—Nine Dimensions of Love* guides you into your own Love Letter Writing Practice. Writing Love Letters *to* and *from* Your Higher Self is a creative act that can be done by anyone who wants to expand his or her experience of love.

Love belongs to you. It is your essence and true nature. As you write your own Love Letters from Your Higher Self, you will feel lighter, freer and more relaxed. Those things that used to knock you off your feet no longer will. Your connection to love at your core grows stronger and feelings of wellbeing and joy emerge for you.

–Small Self and Higher Self–

WE HAVE LIMITED AND RESTRICTED our knowledge of who we really are. We think we are our thoughts, our bodies or our personalities. In truth, we are so much more. We have forgotten our essence – our original nature. It is time to remember and reconnect to the love at our core.

Writing Love Letters *from* Your Higher Self is no small undertaking. To do so, we must expand our self-knowledge. We must awaken beyond our small self to entertain the perspective of our Higher Self. We must wake-up to our own Magnificence and listen deeply to our own inner voice.

–Writing Love Letters–

THE BEST WAY TO START WRITING love letters to and from your Higher Self is to take out a pen and paper and begin. You may feel awkward and uncomfortable at first. As you practice, the words will come.

I have sat with the most talkative of clients who easily share long detailed descriptions of their issues and problems, only to watch their jaws lock when invited to speak one word of love for their Self.

Love has its own language. It does not scold, belittle or condemn. It does not judge, control or diminish. It is patient, considerate and attentive. It carries a distinct tone of kindness. Love cherishes and respects. These are feelings and qualities to reach for in your love letters writing practice.

Writing Love Letters to and from Your Higher Self will help you to:

- Release tension from your nervous system
- Detoxify accumulated stress from your emotional body
- Dissolve faulty thinking and limiting beliefs that hold you back
- Unravel constrictions that inhibit your creative flow
- Heal your addiction to struggle
- Overcome your dependency on external sources for happiness
- Reconnect with your own essence qualities
- Feel genuine joy and peace
- Awaken a still calm center at your core.
- See, feel and love the world as your Higher Self loves.

There is no stopping love from finding us. Love is our essential nature. When we turn in the direction of love, we come home to our Higher Self. Our hearts wake up and love flourishes. Let's begin now.

Part One

LOVE LETTER
WRITING PRACTICES

Love Letter Writing Practices

IT IS ONE THING TO READ *Love Letters From Your Higher Self* and to enjoy comforting waves as words of love surround and soothe you. It is another to cultivate your own, very personal relationship with your Higher Self and to write Love Letters to your self. I intend to help you do that.

Here, you will find a foundational Love Letter Writing Practice. I use this practice myself, as do my clients. If you are willing to devote even a small amount of time to developing your Love Letter Writing Practice, you will soon discover your life enriched and enhanced—from the inside.

Love is ever-present and available to us from our Higher Selves. We know this intellectually. Some days we trust it and other days we doubt. Through these Love Letter Writing Practices, you open a direct inner path to love. Love becomes available to you regardless of any external condition or circumstance.

My own practice in writing Love Letters has evolved over the years. At first, I fumbled to find words. I knew writing brought me comfort and relief and for a long time, that was enough to keep me writing. But as I wrote, I noticed there was more going on than just a purging of emotional tension and a sorting out of inner conflicts. Through my writing, I tapped into wisdom, received guidance and found answers I didn't know I had.

I wrote page after page and at a certain point, I felt a distinct shift. The tone of my writing changed. Although I couldn't put my finger on what was happening, I knew I was writing from a different perspective—outside of my ordinary mind. Instead of thinking about what I wrote, the words just issued forth. I watched as messages formed, guidance came and insights appeared. It was as if an inner teacher, who cared about my development and my fulfillment, spoke to and through me. I began to understand that this information came from my Higher Self.

Regardless of how confused, challenged or upset I may feel when I start writing, once that shift takes place, I view the same situation, issue or problem from a more evolved perspective. I come away from my Love Letter Writing Practice feeling transformed.

I continue to use and expand my Practice and regularly hear a similar thrill from my clients when they access the wisdom of their own Higher Selves through their Love Letters.

Some days, I open my journal, write a quick request for guidance and turn my pen over to my Higher Self. I deliberately get out of the way and immediately words from my Higher Self begin flowing through me. On other days—when I am troubled or under emotional stress—it does not happen so quickly.

On those days, I need to write longer letters *to* my Higher Self. I have things to say before I am ready to ask for help. Usually, I am stuck in one of my "stories," replaying an event, trying to figure it all out or hoping I can make it turn out a different way. When I create a place for my small self to fully express the thoughts and feelings swirling around inside, eventually I run out of steam or grow tired of listening to my stories. At that point, I am ready to hear from my Higher Self.

Letters written back and forth from small self to Higher Self are Love Letters. Through consistent communication, sharing, listening and being heard, an intimate and honest partnership is forged.

Here then, is the Love Letter Writing Practice. I offer it to you at the beginning of this workbook so you can get started writing Love Letters to your self right away.

Please, be easy and gentle with yourself as you develop your Love Letter Writing Practice. You may not immediately feel words of love from your own Higher Self pouring through you. With this practice, you invite contact. If you are consistent, you will cultivate your personal relationship with your own Higher Self. Allow this connection to grow. Be patient and persistent. Your Higher Self is there for you—already fully in love with you and ready to offer guidance and support.

–Love Letter Writing Practice: Step One–
*Love Letters **to** Your Higher Self*

EXPRESS YOUR THOUGHTS AND FEELINGS

IMAGINE YOU ARE POURING YOUR HEART OUT to your very best friend and loving companion. Know you are totally safe to share anything and everything. Your Higher Self does not judge or condemn. Your Higher Self loves you without condition. As you write Love Letters to Your Higher Self, give yourself permission to fully express your thoughts and feelings—to purge and get it all out. Know that your Higher Self listens and receives your letters with compassion, acceptance and patience.

Notice if you find yourself going over the same concerns again and again. That is a natural human tendency. We think if we worry long enough, or ruminate more completely, we'll come up with new solutions. Usually, we just end up replaying our stories over the years with different names and locations. Writing Love letters is different from simple venting.

I suggest you start your Love Letter Writing with an intention to remove blocks and release any resistance you have to love. Love works things out in its own way and transforms us from our core. Trust the beauty and simplicity of this creative process and go for pure self-expression. Get to know your feelings. Be honest about your desires. Self-expression leads to self-knowledge and both are empowering. Love Letters *to* Your Higher Self opens doors far more readily than reasoning things out ever will.

In the midst of expressing your thoughts and feelings, you may sense your Higher Self attempting to slip in with an alternate perspective. Good—allow this to happen. Just be conscious – skip a line and deliberately write the words your Higher Self is offering you. For me, the feeling is like reaching to remember a dream. A fragment comes and, if I relax and open to receive, the whole dream follows.

At some point, you will decide to move on to the second step and write a Love Letter *from* Your Higher Self. You may notice your Small Self resisting this shift. We grow attached to our ordinary perspectives—even when they no longer serve us. You may find your Small Self gets even louder, whining, complaining or justifying its position. This is all fine. Just be aware. Are you writing from your small, ordinary limited perspective, or a higher broader more expanded one? Get to know the difference.

Dive in and see what happens. When in doubt—ask your Higher Self for Guidance. You have a built in support system in the form of your own Higher Self. You cannot go wrong.

–Invocation to Higher Love–

Dear Higher Self,

I am ready to love my self.
I am ready to be a source of love, inspiration and kindness.
I need your perspective.
I open my mind, my heart and my body to love.
I welcome your guidance and your wisdom.
I know that when I feel frightened or worried,
I have trouble feeling or hearing you.
I slow down, and remember that you and I are one.
I release all limiting thoughts of separation and lack.
I choose love. I am ready to see as you see.
I am ready to feel as you feel.
I am ready to think as you think.
I am ready to offer words of love to my self right now.
Thank you for your love and support.
Thank you for holding my hand as I step onto this path with you.
Help me to know that I am worthy. Help me open to joy.
Help me to be both lover and loved.
I am ready to be a conduit for your love. I am ready now.
Teach me to love more than I have ever before loved.
Teach me to know love as you know love.

–A Love Letter *to* My Higher Self–

Dear Higher Self,

_____

_____

_____

_____

_____

_____

_____

_____

_____

_____

_____

_____

_____

_____

_____

_____

_____

_____

_____

_____

_____

_____

_____

_____

_____

_____

_____

_____

_____

_____

_____

_____

_____

_____

_____

_____

_____

_____

_____

_____

(Your Signature)

When you feel complete and are ready
to hear from your Higher Self, proceed to:
–Love Letter Writing Practice: Step Two–
Love Letters *from* Your Higher Self.

–Love Letter Writing Practice: Step Two–
Love Letters from Your Higher Self

OPEN, LISTEN, RECEIVE

WRITING LOVE LETTERS *from* Your Higher Self is a choice. You do it because you know intuitively that connecting with your own higher love and wisdom serves you and it serves others as well.

When we take responsibility for our own happiness and cultivate practices that fill us up from the inside, we enter a world of spiritual maturity. For most of us, it is a stretch that requires our focus.

So, how is it done? Here are a few thoughts for you…

❖ What would you most love to hear from your lover, parents, teachers or friends? Write those words to your self.

❖ Think about the people close to you, the friends you trust and those you know, without any doubt, love you unconditionally. What words have they spoken to you that really made a difference? Write those words to your self.

❖ Are there lines from movies, phrases from books, or lyrics from songs that have touched your heart? Write those words to your self.

❖ Imagine you are the best companion, friend, lover you could ever dream of. What words would you speak to your self?

❖ If you are not sure what to write, begin with this:
"I love you—just the way you are." Write this phrase ten times, or twenty times and let it in to your body and heart. Notice how good it feels to receive these words.

The above suggestions will get you started. The key is not to think about it. Simply relax, allow and let it flow. Writing *Love Letters from Your Higher Self* is like free form dancing. You must get out of your head so the rhythm and the music can take over. The vibration of your Higher Self is much larger, fuller and more expanded than your ordinary consciousness. You must release your grip on reality the way you know it now and let yourself rise to that higher vibration.

The Higher Self is always loving, kind and considerate. If you find yourself blaming, criticizing, scolding or being hard on yourself in any way, return to Step One. Your Small Self is writing so let it have the extra time it needs. Your Higher Self will take over again when you are ready.

Some Higher Selves communicate with humor, others use metaphor, and others use poetry to soothe as they converse. You will find your own style and tone. I guarantee your Higher Self wants to communicate with you and will help you find your way.

–Invocation for Higher Wisdom–
Guidance, Support and Help

Dear Higher Self,

I am ready to receive your guidance, support and love.
Is there anything I need to know right now?
I am open to receiving your help.
Please offer me your words of wisdom and love.
I turn over the pen to you now.
Thank you for your consistent and steady presence in my life.
I am listening.
Please offer me your guidance now.

–A Love Letter *from* My Higher Self–

Dear _____   *(your name here),*

_____

_____

_____

_____

_____

_____

_____

_____

_____

_____

_____

_____

_____

_____

_____

_____

_____

_____

_____

_____

_____

_____

_____

_____

_____

_____

_____

_____

_____

_____

_____

_____

_____

_____

_____

_____

_____

_____

_____

_____

_____

_____

With love,
Your Higher Self

–Love Letter Writing Practice: Step Three–
Love Letters of Appreciation

Complete your letter by writing a few words of appreciation to your Higher Self for whatever you received today. Keep it simple and direct. Relationships grow strong and happy when we offer regular appreciations.

–Invocation of Appreciation–

Dear Higher Self,

Thank you for your loving care.
Thank you for the guidance and comfort you offer me.
Thank you for the words you share.
I am grateful to know that you are here.
I look forward to more time together.
Thank you for reminding me that I am loved
And that I am love.

–Love Letter Writing Practice: Step Three–
Write Your Appreciation

Dear Higher Self,

Thank you.

_____

_____

_____

_____

_____

_____

_____

_____

_____

_____

_____

_____

With love,

_____

(Your Signature)

Part Two

Nine Dimensions
of Love

Nine Dimensions of Love

LET'S BEGIN EXPLORING the Nine Dimensions of Love. As you turn your attention toward each dimension, you receive a Love Letter from Your Higher Self. That letter includes an invitation.

Read about each dimension. Open the invitation offered to you. Explore your thoughts and feelings in your Love Letter Writing Practice. Write as many Love Letters as you want.

At times in my life, I write Love Letters from my Higher Self daily. Love Letter Writing is a personally empowering, creative form of meditation. It allows you to easily deepen your self-knowledge and strengthen your inner contentment.

The Nine Dimensions of Love we explore in this workbook are portals of transformation through which conscious living is born. They unfold in a specific order, awakening dimensions of love within and around you. Feel free to jump around if you find yourself strongly called to a particular dimension. Just don't bypass any of the nine dimensions altogether. Eventually, you will want to awaken love through all of them.

The "Presence" Dimension

— 1 —

**An Invitation to
Love in Current Time.**

As long as you are unable to
access the power of the Now,
every emotional pain that you experience
leaves behind a residue of pain
that lives on in you.

—ECKART TOLLE

–An Invitation to Love in Current Time–
*A Love Letter **from** Your Higher Self*

Dear _____

We love you NOW. This current moment is where love happens. It does not happen yesterday but as a memory; it does not happen tomorrow except as a fantasy. You want "Now love" for it is the only love that will ever satisfy and fulfill you.

We invite you to join us in this moment, in the love that we are. You know what love feels like. You know when you are awake to the love flowing inside of you. You know when you are sleeping and have forgotten love. You know when you are resting in the embrace of love and you know when you are standing separate from it.

Love waits for your return and welcomes you home. Listen deeply to the call. Feel the preciousness of love in your life right now. Be present to it all.

Everything happening in your life in this very moment is orchestrated from love for your remembrance of love.

Breathe deeply.

Pause.

Look around at your physical world and know that everything you see with your physical eyes will one day dissolve. What remains constant, in and through it all, is your eternal self—the love that you are.

Let it all dissolve right now. Imagine this movie is complete and feel the Loving You that rests behind the physical world you view. There, you find your freedom—your presence. There, you already have everything you seek. There, at the center of your self, you know that all is well.

Beyond your dramas and behind your stories, all is quiet and full. We are eternally joined there, riding gentle waves of ecstasy and bliss. Love opens and awakens for you in current time—for that is where love is found.

I love in current time and know

that in this moment—right now

—all is well and all is love.

There is no need to wait for conditions to be right, for other people to speak words you long to hear, or for specific events to take place, before you align with the loving presence in your heart. Please, accept our invitation to love in current time and begin now.

With Love,
Your Higher Self

–Awaken Love in Current Time–

NOTHING HURTS MORE than being stuck in regret over what did not occur or spending our days yearning for what has not yet happened. We miss the wonder of our present moments. We miss being intimate with life itself.

When we are lost in the past or off somewhere in the future, we are not fully present for ourselves right here and right now. This lack of inner presence triggers feelings that we label abandonment, neglect, betrayal and abuse. Most often, we blame our feelings on other people. We don't understand it is our own lack of self-love generating our inner discord. We project. We all do it. We can stay imprisoned in endless loops of blame and judgment, feeling victimized by others or by the conditions of our lives until we awaken love in the *Presence* dimension. "Now" is when we align with our Higher Selves.

This return to self happens in current time. It cannot happen anywhere else. That is why a practice of loving in the presence dimension can be so transformational and empowering. The mind is not used to staying present. It likes to run off—back into the past or ahead into the future. When we awaken love in current time, we train our minds to relax. Love then opens in our hearts and expands.

A Presence Meditation
Awaken Love in Current Time

I am alive,
Right here and right now.
In this present moment,
All is well.
I witness and observe my life.
I am present to it all.
I am the presence of love behind and through it all.
I relax into the core of love that I am.

Explore The "Presence" Dimension
In Your Love Letters Writing Practice

Use your first Love Letter *to* your Higher Self to expand your ability to be present right now. Here are some questions for you to consider.

- What are you aware of?
- Where is your attention drawn?
- What is most alive in your awareness right now?
- What are you curious about?
- What troubles or concerns you?
- What would you like to change?
- What do you desire and hope for?
- What delights you?
- What or who do you appreciate?
- What do you wonder about?
- What questions do you have?

This is your Love Letter Writing Practice. Make it your own. Ask your Higher Self to share wisdom that will help you see your world in a positive way right now. Allow your Higher Self to teach and guide you to experience your life in current time.

–A Love Letter *to* My Higher Self–

Dear Higher Self,

_____

_____

_____

_____

_____

_____

_____

_____

_____

_____

_____

_____

_____

_____

_____

_____

_____

_____

_____

_____

_____

_____

_____

_____

_____

_____

_____

_____

_____

_____

_____

_____

_____

_____

_____

_____

_____

_____

_____

_____

_____

_____

_____

_____

_____

_____

_____

_____

_____

(Your Signature)

–A Love Letter *from* My Higher Self–

Dear _____   *(your name here),*

_____

_____

_____

_____

_____

_____

_____

_____

_____

_____

_____

_____

_____

_____

_____

_____

_____

_____

_____

_____

_____

_____

_____

_____

_____

_____

_____

_____

_____

_____

_____

_____

_____

_____

_____

_____

_____

_____

_____

_____

_____

_____

_____

_____

_____

_____

_____

_____

_____

_____

(Your Signature)

–My Appreciations–

Dear Higher Self,

    Thank you.

_____

_____

_____

_____

_____

_____

_____

_____

_____

_____

_____

_____

_____

With love,

_____

(Your Signature)

The "Acceptance" Dimension

— 2 —

**An Invitation to
Love your Body and your Sensations.**

The first duty of love—is to listen.

—PAUL TILLICH

–An Invitation to Love Your Body and Your Sensations–
A Love Letter from Your Higher Self

Dear _____

You body is amazing. Through it, you taste, touch, see, hear, smell and receive the wonders of the physical world. Waves of sensation crash over you as you dance, sing, hike in the forest, walk barefoot on the beach, play sports, create art and, of course—when you make-love.

Your mental body offers you the gift of thought. Your emotional body provides a wide range of feeling. Through your physical body, you experience the great expanse of glorious sensations. How amazing you and your perceptions are. We invite you to accept your body and your sensations fully.

We love your sensations—and we invite you to love them as well. Drink in the deliciousness of life. Let the wind caress you. Let rain delight you. Let sunshine warm you. Let colors tingle through you, music dance into you and enjoy the rich sensual tapestry of your life. We don't want you to miss any of it.

Everything in the world thrives on loving acceptance and nurturing. That includes your body and the sensations it awakens in you.

Join us in celebration of your physical life. Take a walk in nature and sense the beauty. Visit a flower shop and find a scent that pleases you. Listen to music and let the sounds sweep their magic into you. Eat a meal and savor each bite. Softly pet your animal. Hold hands with your lover. Move your body with sensuality and pleasure.

Love and accept your body, and all of your sensations. You will be surprised at the level of health and vitality you experience in your body, when you choose to accept your physical life fully.

Today, we invite you to love your body and your sensations as we do.

I love and accept my body and my sensations.

As you offer loving acceptance, stored toxins of self-judgment are tossed away from your mental body. Your nervous system releases its shame and grief. Your whole body opens and clears. You are not your body. You are the consciousness within your body. You are not your sensations. You are the consciousness experiencing your sensations. We invite you to accept it all today.

With Love,
Your Higher Self

–Awaken Love for your Body and Sensations–

MOST OF US ARE CONVINCED something is wrong or is about to be wrong with our bodies. If all is well today, we are sure we will "pick up" something bad tomorrow.

The body is incredibly resilient. It knows how to do so many things we cannot imagine or figure out with our minds alone. The sensations arising in our bodies enrich our enjoyment of the physical world. Often, we take these feelings for granted.

For some, the immense range of sensations we experience is overwhelming and frightening. Accepting the innocence of our bodies and the sensations that flow through them requires trust. Trust in the natural order of life, and trust in a perfect unfolding adventure for us here in the physical world.

When we love our bodies and our sensations, we bathe our cells with safety. When we have trouble loving our bodies, we generate distress instead. Writing Love Letters to our Higher Self, with a focus on loving our bodies and sensations, awakens a quality of love that many of us shy away from. We identify so directly with our bodies, loving them seems confusing at first. We have physical bodies. We are not our physical bodies. We are the consciousness—the presence—awake in and through the body. Let's practice bringing loving acceptance to our bodies and sensations today and everyday.

An Acceptance Meditation
Awaken Love for Your Sensations and Your Body

I have a body. I am not my body.
I am the consciousness animating my physical body.
I choose to love my body exactly as it is,
As I relax into the core of love that is the real me.

I have sensations. I am not my sensations.
I am the consciousness experiencing sensations.
I choose to love my sensations and let them be,
As I relax into the core of love that is the real me.

Explore The "Acceptance" Dimension
In Your Love Letters Writing Practice

In your next Love Letters offer love to your body and to your sensations. Here are some questions for you to consider as you begin. Remember these are your love letters to your own inner being and Spirit. You are free to say anything and everything.

- How do you feel about your body?

- How do you express love to your body?

- What sensations are you aware of in your body?

- What do you notice when you taste, touch, smell, see, hear and sense your physical world right now?

- What words might you use to express love to your body?

- What words might you use to celebrate your human senses?

- What else needs acceptance?

- What words of acceptance do you long to hear? Offer them to yourself right now.

Acceptance is one of the keys to transformation. Once we accept ourselves - exactly as we are right now—we are empowered for change. Fighting against "what is" only depletes our energy. If you feel frustration or have difficulty accepting your physical body—as many of us do—make a decision to generate more love for yourself. Set your intention to fully accept yourself and find the words that soothe and comfort your body right now. Ask your Higher Self to help you.

–A Love Letter *to* My Higher Self–

Dear Higher Self,

_____

_____

_____

_____

_____

_____

_____

_____

_____

_____

_____

_____

_____

_____

_____

_____

_____

_____

_____

_____

_____

_____

_____

_____

_____

_____

_____

_____

_____

_____

_____

_____

_____

_____

_____

_____

_____

_____

_____

_____

_____

_____

_____

_____

_____

_____

_____

(Your Signature)

−A Love Letter *from* My Higher Self−

Dear _____   *(your name here),*

_____

_____

_____

_____

_____

_____

_____

_____

_____

_____

_____

_____

_____

_____

_____

_____

_____

_____

_____

_____

_____

_____

_____

_____

_____

_____

_____

_____

_____

_____

_____

_____

_____

_____

_____

_____

_____

_____

_____

_____

_____

_____

_____

_____

_____

(Your Signature)

—My Appreciations—

Dear Higher Self,

Thank you.

_____

_____

_____

_____

_____

_____

_____

_____

_____

_____

_____

_____

_____

_____

With love,

_____

(Your Signature)

The "Energy" Dimension

— 3 —

**An Invitation to
Love your Feelings.**

.

The trick is in what one emphasizes.
We either make ourselves miserable,
or we make ourselves happy.
The amount of work is the same.
—CARLOS CASTANEDA

–An Invitation to Love Your Feelings–
A Love Letter from Your Higher Self

Dear _____

We want you to know we would never withhold our love from you. Not ever, no matter what you are feeling. Inclusion is the order of the Universe and the true nature of your own heart.

You have a whole range of feelings and the feeling realm is where energy flows into motion for you. When you allow and embrace all of your emotions, you open your inner space for passion and bliss. As you love your lower feelings, you help yourself stretch to make room for higher ones.

We know you decided that some of your feelings are acceptable and others are not. In truth, your feelings are like children—each one unique and precious. You know, deep in your heart that all children and all feelings deserve love. We love you and all of your feelings like that.

We invite you to extend love to ALL your emotions. We invite you to love them as we do. You will discover there are no monsters waiting for you either high up or down low. In truth, you have just as much difficulty loving feelings of ecstasy as you do feelings of sorrow. We know that you frighten yourself with thoughts about your emotions. You tell yourself that they will overwhelm you.

"Overwhelmed" is just another feeling that needs your love. Your feelings are moving energy. They enliven, guide and inspire you. Love all of your feelings completely. This does not mean you need to linger or become stuck in any one emotion. Let them flow—the way children flow from one feeling to another.

Today, we invite you to celebrate the energy of your feelings as we do.

I offer love to all of my feelings and I let them be.

We love you in and through all dimensions of your existence and that includes the Energy Dimension, the dimension of feelings. We are that much in love with you.

It is time to awaken as the divine lover that you are. This is our invitation to you. Relax and know the positive flow of energy that comes from loving all of your feelings.

With Love,
Your Higher Self

–Practice Loving your Feelings–

MOST OF US, AT TIMES, feel victim to our emotions. Instead of riding their currents and letting them wash easily through us, we resist, fight, deny, minimize, ignore, neglect or attempt to suppress them. Pushing feelings away however, does nothing to erase them.

Many of us live with the mistaken idea that in connecting with our Higher Self and becoming, "more spiritual," we will never again feel sad, lonely or frustrated. True spirituality embraces and accepts the full range of human experience. The key is not to stop feeling, but to retrieve the messages of our feelings and to ride the waves of our energy to ever more positive feelings.

We did not come here to avoid living or feeling. Let us build our stamina for an energetic life. Let us open wide our arms and our hearts to the magic and the majesty of our human feelings. There, we find great passion and inspiration. Let us know, once and for all, we are not broken, or bruised when sadness or frustration washes through us.

Our hurts and fears are transformed when we love our feelings. Instead of blocking the flow of our essence—we feel energy dancing through us.

An Energy Meditation
Awaken Love for Your Feelings

I have feelings.
I am not my feelings.
I am the loving energy in and through all of my feelings.
I choose to love my feelings and let them be,
As I relax into the core of love that is the real me.

Explore The "Energy" Dimension
In Your Love Letters Writing Practice

Feelings are energy. They are fuel for your dreams. Give yourself permission to express your feelings here. Give each feeling a voice. Let your feelings have room in your life. They are important and they belong to you.

- Tell your Higher Self exactly how you feel.

- You can use this Love Letters Writing Practice to explore your feelings, and receive guidance about the four major rooms of your life:

  ❖ How do you feel about HEALTH?
  ❖ How do you feel about WEALTH?
  ❖ How do you feel about WORK AND PLAY?
  ❖ How do you feel about LOVE?

Ask your Higher Self to help you create what you want to feel in each area of your life. You have support and inner guidance. You also have a direct connection to the creative forces of the Universe. As you cultivate this connection you learn to Dance with the Universe. Your Higher Self is your dance partner and there are many dances to learn and enjoy.

–A Love Letter *to* My Higher Self–

Dear Higher Self,

_____

_____

_____

_____

_____

_____

_____

_____

_____

_____

_____

_____

_____

_____

_____

_____

_____

_____

_____

_____

_____

_____

(Your Signature)

–A Love Letter *from* My Higher Self–

Dear _____ *(your name here),*

_____

_____

_____

_____

_____

_____

_____

_____

_____

_____

_____

_____

_____

_____

_____

_____

_____

_____

_____

_____

_____

_____

_____

_____

_____

_____

_____

_____

_____

_____

_____

_____

_____

_____

_____

_____

_____

_____

_____

_____

_____

_____

_____

_____

_____

_____

_____

_____

_____

_____

_____

(Your Signature)

–My Appreciations–

Dear Higher Self,

Thank you.

_____

_____

_____

_____

_____

_____

_____

_____

_____

_____

_____

_____

_____

_____

_____

_____

With love,

_____

(Your Signature)

The "Focus" Dimension

— 4 —

**An Invitation to
Love your Thoughts.**

*Love has the power of making you believe
what you would normally treat with the deepest suspicion.*
—MIRABEAU

–An Invitation to Love Your Thoughts–
A Love Letter from Your Higher Self

Dear _____

Your thoughts are not your enemies, though you often act as if they are. Clearly, many of your thoughts are not the friendliest of allies. When you take your thoughts as the truth about you, and go to battle with them, the result is inner conflict, confusion and despair.

We invite you to first make friends with your thoughts and then to focus them in loving ways. Your thoughts are powerful but do not deceive yourself. You are much more powerful. And you—the choice maker, director, and producer of your thoughts—are invited today to focus and formulate ongoing loving thoughts for yourself, for your life and for others.

Today, we want to shine our light on your ability to focus and extend love through your thoughts. There are only two things required from you:

- ***Release your preoccupation with right and wrong, good and bad, and all thoughts that separate.***

- ***Relax into your own heart.***

Notice, we do not suggest that you stop thinking. We ask that you relax your preoccupation and obsession with certain forms of thinking and make a choice to focus your thoughts in loving ways.

Love is the most powerful healer of all. By infusing your thoughts with love, you activate relief and generate power in your mental body.

We invite you to open this empowering dimension of focus. Relax into it. Rest easy in love and let the dramatic and stormy nature of your thoughts dance, diminish and dissolve.

We love you in and through all dimensions of your existence including your thoughts. We are that much in love with you.

Today, we invite you to love your thoughts and to focus them to see love, know love and be love.

I love my thoughts and
focus them in loving ways.

We love your thoughts without conflict or resistance. We love you completely.

With Love,
Your Higher Self

−Practice Loving your Thoughts−

IN MY YEARS AS A MENTOR, counselor and healing practitioner, there is one thing, more than anything else that consistently brings calm to the mental body and to our entire human energy system. That thing is love. Love is, by far, the greatest healer in existence.

Our thoughts are like frightened and disoriented children, searching for safety. They need the gentle loving care we offer when we consciously align with and express love from our hearts. When children feel loved, a core of inner stability and peace is established inside them. The same is true of us—regardless of our age—when we think loving thoughts.

To focus our thoughts in loving ways, we must detach from them long enough to observe them. We need to remember that we have thoughts but we are not our thoughts. When we do this, we shift our perspective. Negative thoughts diminish in the light of a consciousness deliberately focused on love.

Skill with the Focus Dimension of Love is essential for achieving fulfillment in the other dimensions. Use your Love Letter Writing Practice to gain awareness of your ordinary thoughts and then choose to focus your thoughts with love and for love.

A Focus Meditation
Awaken Love through Your Thoughts

I have thoughts.
I am not my thoughts.
I am the consciousness behind and through all of my thinking.
The consciousness that I am is Love.
I choose to love my thoughts and to focus love through my thoughts,
As I relax into the core of love that is the real me.

Explore The "Focus" Dimension
In Your Love Letters Writing Practice

Thoughts are powerful. They direct our energy and generate our feelings. The thoughts we are conscious of are only one part of the story. It is the unconscious thoughts that carry our history and the decisions we made long ago that may or may not serve us anymore.

- What thoughts drag you down?
- What thoughts lift you up?
- What thoughts inspire you?
- What thoughts diminish you?
- What thoughts would you like to focus upon?

Your Love Letters writing practice will help you know your thoughts. It will give you an opportunity to choose positive uplifting thoughts. Ask your Higher Self to help you view your life from a more expanded perspective. Ask your Higher Self to help you choose loving thoughts that feel good in your body and in your heart. Ask you Higher Self to help you release thoughts that don't serve you anymore.

–A Love Letter *to* My Higher Self–

Dear Higher Self,

_____

_____

_____

_____

_____

_____

_____

_____

_____

_____

_____

_____

_____

_____

_____

_____

_____

_____

_____

_____

_____

_____

_____

_____

_____

_____

_____

_____

_____

_____

_____

_____

_____

_____

_____

_____

_____

_____

_____

_____

_____

_____

_____

_____

_____

_____

(Your Signature)

–A Love Letter *from* My Higher Self–

Dear _____ *(your name here),*

_____

_____

_____

_____

_____

_____

_____

_____

_____

_____

_____

_____

_____

_____

_____

_____

_____

_____

_____

_____

_____

_____

_____

_____

_____

_____

_____

_____

_____

_____

_____

_____

_____

_____

_____

_____

_____

_____

_____

_____

_____

_____

_____

_____

_____

_____

(Your Signature)

–My Appreciations–

Dear Higher Self,

Thank you.

_____

_____

_____

_____

_____

_____

_____

_____

_____

_____

_____

_____

_____

With love,

_____

(Your Signature)

The "Connection" Dimension

— 5 —

An Invitation to
Love the Cast of Characters in Your Life.

For when I can love all of me,
I will love all of you.
—DEBBIE FORD

All violence is the result of people tricking themselves
into believing that their pain derives from other people
and that consequently those people deserve to be punished.
—MARSHALL ROSENBERG

–An Invitation to Love the Cast of Characters in Your Life–
A Love Letter from Your Higher Self

Dear _____

We love you and all the many facetted expressions of you. As we bring our love to you in this letter, we ask you to consider... How would your world be different if you knew that every single person you encountered was not someone separate from you? Each character in the movie of your life enacts another aspect of you. It is time for you to burst through the illusion of separation into the truth of your loving connection to everyone and everything.

Truly, you encounter an exquisite cast of characters within the course of your days. A multi-facetted cast of characters is what you are—all by yourself—even if you never leave your own bedroom.

When you look upon yourself and the people in your life with love, you see them as we do, each a prism of color within the total light of existence.

There is no separation between you and anything that appears in your experience. We know this is often difficult for you to fathom. Even when you grasp the concept, it is a challenge for you to accept—especially when the people closest to you do things you imagine you would never do.

Don't try to figure out the whole cosmos today. Simply love and connect. Open your heart and be the lover that you are. Love the cast of characters in your life and let them be. Love all of them—fully. This does not mean you need to kiss everyone who crosses your path, or spend time with them, or even speak to them. You need only to rest in the love that you are and acknowledge that you are connected to everyone you encounter.

I love the entire cast of
characters in my life and know that
we are connected in love.

We love you completely—all parts of you. We invite you to love the entire cast of characters in your life. That includes all parts of your self and all those who appear to be separate from you. Love in the Connection Dimension transforms your relationships and provides you with the peace you seek.

With Love,
Your Higher Self

–Love the Cast of Characters in Your Life–
... and know them as your reflections.

THIS IS, PERHAPS, the most difficult Dimension of Love for most of us to grasp. While we long to feel deeply connected to each other, we have learned our safety comes through defining and maintaining our separateness. To feel safe, unique and connected all at once, challenges our carefully constructed "us and them" perception of reality. But, the truth is simple: Connection joins us. Separation divides.

It is far easier for us to love those who demonstrate qualities we admire and aspire to—much more difficult to feel connected to those whose behavior appears foreign or distasteful to us. While we are quick to justify our lack of love by outlining the character defects of others, we cringe inside because our Higher Selves know that what we see in others is true in ourselves as well.

I have a friend who consistently teaches me about the Connection Dimension of Love. I witness her consistent love for the cast of characters in her life and I am awed. When and if thoughts of judgment, criticism or condemnation rise in her mind, she takes those thoughts into the cauldron of her heart and transforms them. She knows connection is her true nature and she is committed to it.

Do you have a gifted lover in your cast of characters too? We learn so much about our own capacity for love when we see love flowing through others. There are angels among us who show us what love really is. We would be wise to pay attention.

A Connection Meditation

Awaken Love for Everyone

I love the Cast of Characters in my life.
I see each character as a reflection,
Demonstrating a different aspect of who I am.
I am the consciousness and energy of love,
Expressing as all the characters in my life.
The consciousness that I am is Love.
I choose to love all the characters in my life and let them be,
As I relax into the core of love that is the real me.

Explore The "Connection" Dimension
In Your Love Letters Writing Practice

Loving others—especially those who push our buttons—is an inside job. No outer action is required from you. In your Love Letters writing practice you are learning to love the cast of characters in your life as your reflections. Everyone you encounter helps you to love your self more. Once you fill your own inner cup, loving others will come naturally. Your relationships will be lighter and fuller too.

We do this writing practice for our self because we want freedom and peace. Living in conflict with others hurts. Releasing resentments, justifications and the need to be right opens the door for genuine connections.

- Who is easy for you to love and why?

- Who is difficult for you to love and why?

- How might you see your more challenging relationships in a new way?

These three questions will give you plenty to write about! Remember to ask your Higher Self for guidance. We get stuck seeing people through the eyes of our past experiences and expectations. Our Higher Selves see others through the eyes of love. When we release our small mind perspective we are often surprised by what we discover.

–A Love Letter *to* My Higher Self–

Dear Higher Self,

_____

_____

_____

_____

_____

_____

_____

_____

_____

_____

_____

_____

_____

_____

_____

_____

_____

_____

_____

_____

_____

_____

_____

_____

_____

_____

_____

_____

_____

_____

_____

_____

_____

_____

_____

_____

_____

_____

_____

_____

_____

_____

_____

_____

_____

_____

_____

_____

_____

_____

_____

(Your Signature)

–A Love Letter *from* My Higher Self–

Dear _____ *(your name here),*

_____

_____

_____

_____

_____

_____

_____

_____

_____

_____

_____

_____

_____

_____

_____

_____

_____

_____

_____

_____

_____

_____

_____

_____

_____

_____

_____

_____

_____

_____

_____

_____

_____

_____

_____

_____

_____

_____

_____

_____

_____

_____

_____

_____

_____

_____

_____

_____

_____

_____

_____

(Your Signature)

–My Appreciations–

Dear Higher Self,

Thank you.

_____

_____

_____

_____

_____

_____

_____

_____

_____

_____

_____

_____

_____

_____

_____

With love,

_____

(Your Signature)

The "Expression" Dimension

— 6 —

**An Invitation to
Love Your Uniqueness.**

*It is indeed extremely unlikely
that two complex snowflakes will look exactly alike.
It's so extremely unlikely, in fact,
that even if you looked at every one ever made
you would not find any exact duplicates.*
—PHYSICIST KENNETH G. LIBBRECHT

–An Invitation to Love Your Uniqueness–
A Love Letter from Your Higher Self

Dear _____

There is no other like you. That is the truth. Just as unique snowflakes are formed from the same elements, you emerge from the same essential life force as everyone else.

Right now, inside of you, the seeds of unexpressed potentials exist in various states of gestation, en route to their realization and fulfillment. We know this both excites and terrifies you. You came with a personal purpose and creative intention that you long to fulfill. We love you and we are here to help and support you on this adventure.

We know you often wonder how to express your uniqueness. It all starts with this: tell yourself the truth about what you really desire. You must know what you want.

Allow yourself to know what you want, right now, in this moment. Let your desires rise fully into your awareness. Notice what feelings come with them. If you feel joy, enthusiasm and inspiration, you are aligning with your uniqueness. If you feel anything less than full delight and happiness, you are bumping up against your own resistance to being your fullest and most distinctive self.

Everything is unfolding perfectly, allowing you to breakthrough your resistance. When you love your uniqueness as we do, your resistance dissolves, revealing your exceptionality and opening the Expression Dimension.

We want to comfort you today. We know your dreams and your deepest purpose. We carry them for you in their fulfilled state, even when you forget how deeply you long for them to be realized. You truly can relax and enjoy your journey. Your uniqueness is assured along with the fulfillment of your dreams. You already are the magnificence you seek. You—and your desires—are completely formed in Spirit. You came to enjoy their expression in physical form.

We invite you to trust your creative process and to love your uniqueness.

I love my unique expressions.

Tell yourself the truth about what you desire, where you are headed and who you are. Honor and respect your uniqueness as we do. Love waters the seeds of potential within you and helps you to flourish.

With Love,
Your Higher Self

–Awaken Love for Your Uniqueness–
... give yourself permission to express freely

UNLESS WE WERE RAISED IN FAMILIES that celebrated differences and supported unique expressiveness, most of us squashed or withheld our creative impulses long ago. Regardless of our early experiences, the prevalent cultural mindset we live in asks us to conform in order to belong. In our hearts, we long to fit in. We crave the acceptance that comes from being part of a group or crowd.

That is why self-love sets us free. When we provide ourselves with the acceptance we seek, we no longer need to hold back our distinctiveness. Courage, commitment and confidence are by-products of self-love.

According to the Law of Attraction, the vibration we attain on the inside attracts to us the same on the outside. Like attracts like. This is true in my life. When I squash my own creativity, I attract others who see my uniqueness as a threat to our relationship. As I practice love for my uniqueness and risk creative expression without worrying what others think, I attract those who celebrate what I do. Those relationships flourish with shared enthusiasm and mutual respect.

Loving our uniqueness is an act of courage, and a form of self-proclamation. This is who I am. Like it, love it or leave it. I stand in love behind and for myself. As we fall in love with our self we open the expression dimension and are empowered to enjoy the creative unfolding of our lives.

Please, explore your love for your uniqueness in your next Love Letters Writing Practice.

An Expression Meditation

Awaken love for your creative freedom

I am unique, whole and free.
I have a unique vision and creative purpose for being.
I choose to love my uniqueness
And to express it fully,
As I create from the Love
That is the essence of me.

Explore The "Expression" Dimension

In Your Love Letters Writing Practice

Here are a few questions to ask:

- What is unique about you?

- What do you long to express?

- What holds you back?

- Do you compare yourself to others?

- Do you limit your expression around certain people?

- Where do you feel most free to express yourself?

- What would you like to express right now?

- What words of love would be helpful to you right now?

We all need to know that we are lovable just the way we are. Use your next Love Letter *to Your Higher Self* to express yourself. Ask your Higher Self to encourage, support and guide you in your self-expression. Ask your Higher Self to offer you guidance, encouragement and support.

If you feel wobbly about expressing yourself ask your Higher Self for words of confidence and courage. If you feel shy about expressing yourself ask your Higher Self for words of self-respect and celebration. If you feel excited to express yourself ask your Higher Self to add energy and inspiration to carry you into your unique dance of expression.

—A Love Letter *to* My Higher Self—

Dear Higher Self,

_____

_____

_____

_____

_____

_____

_____

_____

_____

_____

_____

_____

_____

_____

_____

_____

_____

_____

_____

_____

_____

_____

_____

_____

_____

_____

_____

_____

_____

_____

_____

_____

_____

_____

_____

_____

_____

_____

_____

_____

_____

_____

_____

_____

_____

_____

_____

_____

_____

(Your Signature)

–A Love Letter *from* My Higher Self–

Dear _____   *(your name here),*

_____

_____

_____

_____

_____

_____

_____

_____

_____

_____

_____

_____

_____

_____

_____

_____

_____

_____

_____

_____

_____

_____

_____

_____

_____

_____

(Your Signature)

—My Appreciations—

Dear Higher Self,

   Thank you.

_____

_____

_____

_____

_____

_____

_____

_____

_____

_____

_____

_____

With love,

_____

(Your Signature)

The "Intuition" Dimension

— 7 —

**An Invitation to
Love your Visions.**

Love is what we are born with.
Fear is what we learn.
The spiritual journey is the unlearning of fear and prejudices
and the acceptance of love back in our hearts.
Love is the essential reality and our purpose on earth.
To be consciously aware of it,
to experience love in ourselves and others,
is the meaning of life.
Meaning does not lie in things.
Meaning lies in us.

—MARIANNE WILLIAMSON

–An Invitation to Love Your Visions–
A Love Letter from Your Higher Self

Dear _____

There is nothing wrong. We promise you that. No matter what your life looks like, nothing wrong is taking place in your world today. The Universe is working in your favor, on your behalf, to inspire your visions and their fulfillment.

What prevents you from loving your whole life and everything in it? Do you think there is something "wrong" with the events that occur and the people and things that show up in your life? That thought blocks your intuition and diminishes your creative power.

When you bump up against something you think should not be occurring, you contract. The truth is, in contraction you discover your preferences and are better able to define your visions. Contraction is not bad. It serves a specific purpose. However, staying contracted is a choice and today we invite you to make a higher choice. Move through your contractions to embrace your greatest visions for your life. That is something we are always doing for you. You are not stuck or alone. We deliver messages to you through your intuitive body.

We are here. Love is present as the undercurrent of every single experience and event in your world. As you open the Intuition Dimension of Love, our whispers of wisdom come to you as pulses of inner knowledge.

We invite you into your greatest vision for your life. Open your intuition. You do this by looking into the eyes of adversity and reminding yourself that, here too, love is present. There is no place where love is absent. Expand through current conditions and reach for your vision. We are here guiding you.

Trusting your intuition is a choice. Your greatest visions are born here. We invite you forward. We know the unfolding of your visions for you.

I love my expanding visions and trust my intuitions.

If you could see through our eyes, you would see love dancing before you in a festival of events and sounds. Indeed, you can see through our eyes for inner sight belongs to you. We invite you to love your visions and to trust your intuitions.

We love you,
Your Higher Self

–Love Your Visions and Listen to Your Intuitions–

ONE OF THE MOST STUBBORN habits of thought we have difficulty surrendering, is the belief that something is essentially wrong with life. Most of us do senseless battle with our life circumstances and conditions—an act as futile as fighting the weather.

In our attempt to control life, we miss or ignore the intuitive signals that would naturally lead us to better experiences. We suffer endlessly until we realize control is not what life is about. We get stuck.

Looking back adds fuel to what has already happened. Looking forward—from now—allows us to expand our vision. When we recognize and value our intuitions we align with our Higher Self and whole new vistas open up.

It is a wonderful practice to listen to our gut hunches, to admit what we already know, and to honor our intuitions through our actions. Love letter writing practices help us tap into the intuition dimension. We deliberately turn toward the invisible wisdom that rests behind ordinary appearances. There we uncover our truth. Moment-to-moment we grow more fine-tuned and awake.

An Intuition Meditation

I am alive with infinite possibilities.
I trust the unfolding of my visions.
I listen to the call of my Higher Self,
Guiding me toward my own fulfillment.
I trust my intuitions and follow them.

Explore The "Intuition" Dimension
In Your Love Letters Writing Practice

Explore your intuitions in your next Love Letters writing practice. Your intuitions are powerful signals that will guide you on your own course through life. Here are some questions to help you explore the Intuition dimension:

- What do you already know?
- What do you "sense" or "intuit" is true for you?
- What are your dreams telling you?
- What whispers of guidance do you hear?
- What gut feelings do you have?
- What does your Higher Self know for you?

Ask your Higher Self for guidance and input on any area of your life. You will feel a "click" or "resonance" in your energy body as you write and hit upon something especially important. Listen as you write. Get out of the way and let your Higher Self deliver love to you in the form of inner messages.

When we get comfortable trusting and following our intuitions we have an inner compass that makes decision making easy. Life gets simpler and we Dance with the Universe more often.

–A Love Letter *to* My Higher Self–

Dear Higher Self,

_____
_____
_____
_____
_____
_____
_____
_____
_____
_____
_____
_____
_____
_____
_____
_____
_____
_____
_____
_____
_____
_____
_____
_____
_____

_____

_____

_____

_____

_____

_____

_____

_____

_____

_____

_____

_____

_____

_____

_____

_____

_____

_____

_____

_____

_____

_____

_____

(Your Signature)

–A Love Letter *from* My Higher Self–

Dear _____   *(your name here),*

_____

_____

_____

_____

_____

_____

_____

_____

_____

_____

_____

_____

_____

_____

_____

_____

_____

_____

_____

_____

_____

_____

_____

(Your Signature)

–My Appreciations–

Dear Higher Self,

Thank you.

_____

_____

_____

_____

_____

_____

_____

_____

_____

_____

_____

_____

_____

With love,

_____

(Your Signature)

The "Wholeness" Dimension

— 8 —

**An Invitation to
Love your Fullness and Your Money**

*People with a scarcity mentality
tend to see everything in terms of win-lose.
There is only so much; and if someone else has it,
that means there will be less for me.
The more principle-centered we become,
the more we develop an abundance mentality,
the more we are genuinely happy for the successes,
well-being, achievements, recognition,
and good fortune of other people.
We believe their success adds to...
rather than detracts from... our lives.*

—STEPHEN R. COVEY

–An Invitation to Love Your Fullness and Your Money–
A Love Letter from Your Higher Self

Dear _____

We planned to write you a love letter inviting you to join us in loving your fullness. But, we saw that you cannot get close to experiencing your own completeness, when you are convinced that you are lacking. This shows up most clearly in the state of your bank account. So, we decided to help you open to this Wholeness Dimension of Love through the route that would be the most direct for you. We invite you to love your money.

Attempting to love your fullness, while ignoring the lack you feel about money, is like trying to bypass a bear in your kitchen to get to the refrigerator. It is much better to love the bear and offer it some honey.

You have a choice to make here and it is a big one. We offer it to you through a steady flow of loving messages. You are full. You are whole. You are connected to an abundant Universe. There is nothing you are lacking.

The choice we allude to is this: You can choose to have your experience of fullness be dependent upon external circumstances. This means you will be tossed about on waves of ever changing emotional and financial weather systems. Or, you can choose to rest in the core of love, ever-present within you, and know the true state of fullness that is your essential nature. In this case and with this choice, your acceptance of your essential fullness attracts more fullness to you. And, a demonstration of that is the flow of more money.

We know this is a radical shift of perception for you. Let us assure you it is one you are truly ready for. We celebrate this time of awakening and the fact that you are reading our words of love in this moment.

It is time to break free of the chains that link your happiness to the amount of money in your purse or wallet. Consider loving money, without requiring it to be a specific amount.

When your bank account is full, you feel full as well. When your bank account is empty, you are convinced that you are empty and lacking. Much of your experience of wholeness hinges on the flow of money in your life. This is keeping you from soaring with the freedom and joy that belongs to you. It is this dependency upon external conditions, restricting the flow of money toward you.

We love you and we want to help liberate you from this restriction. We invite you to remember the fullness that is your true nature. To open this Wholeness Dimension, we invite you to know fullness and to love your money, regardless of quantity. Take one penny, a jar of quarters or a handful of paper dollars and love them. Do you know what will happen? Your money will stop being a reason for you to feel bad. Instead of generating stress and conflict, that only attracts more stress and conflict (often in the form of money problems); you will reconnect with the love that emanates from your innate fullness. Your bank accounts might empty out because you are having such a great time spending and sharing your wealth, but they will quickly refill as you relax in your own fullness.

When you think about money, does a smile come to your face? Or, do you feel tightness in your belly and tension in your neck? We invite you to make loving your money a daily practice. Once you are smiling each time you think about money, extend this to your bills and all your expenses. Love them all. Delight in the flow of money—in and out—like steadily pulsing waves on a tropical shoreline.

When loving your money becomes a relaxed practice, additional aspects of this wholeness dimension open for you as well. You are full. We invite you to feel your fullness and love it. Does that mean you lack nothing? That's right. You lack nothing. We know your mind will have a huge debate with this idea, but your heart knows. Come to your heart now. Come home to love.

I love my money. I am whole and full.

Offer love to your money and know you are full. All is well in this moment, regardless of how much you seem to have. You have it all. You are whole. We know this for you.

With Love,
Your Higher Self

–Love Your Fullness and Your Money–
...remember that you are whole.

WHEN I FIRST RECEIVED the Love Letter from Your Higher Self for this Whole Person Dimension, I was surprised. For a few years now, I have been following the guidance of my Higher Self and deliberately cultivating a feeling of fullness each time I write a check or look at my bank statement. Initially, I thought this practice was personalized for me. I took my self to the edge financially so many times in my life and needed to transform my approach to money. I did not understand how common it is to be stuck within a fixed illusion of lack.

A few people in my life appear to have no "money" issues. However, as I get to know them better, I see that even these people fear losing what they have, are concerned about mis-using their wealth, or wonder if their financial comfort puts a damper on their enthusiasm and drive for deeper life fulfillment.

The Wholeness Dimension is where our human personality aligns with Spirit. We are both physically oriented and spiritually resourceful. When we forget we are—in essence—whole and full, we cut ourselves off from our unlimited Universal resources. When we embody full-ness, magic happens and the flow of abundance increases and floods us with riches.

Please, take this Wholeness Dimension of Love to heart. Train your mind to remember fullness. Don't let yourself off the hook on this one. It takes diligence and commitment to breakthrough such a strongly ingrained mindset of lack. When you do, the doors of Abundance are flung open. Not only does money begin to flow, but we tap into clarity, joy and enthusiasm for whole life fulfillment as well.

A Wholeness Meditation

Awaken love for Fullness

I am full, whole and complete.
I am the consciousness and energy of fullness
That expresses as wealth in all areas of life.
The consciousness that I am is full.
I choose to know fullness, to love my money
And to know that I am Whole and
Connected to an endless abundant flow.

Explore The "Wholeness" Dimension

In Your Love Letters Writing Practice

One of the most direct ways into the Wholeness dimension is by cleaning up our thoughts and feelings about money. As you write your Love Letters notice whenever you are expressing thoughts or feelings of lack or not enough. Dive in to this process fully and face your money issues.

- What does money mean to you?
- What is your definition of wealth?
- Do you love money?
- Do you push money away?
- Do you welcome money into your life?
- What do you tell yourself about money?
- How do you feel when you pay your bills?
- What would help you to feel full inside?
- What words of love would help?
- What does your Higher Self know for you?

Ask your Higher Self to help you clean up your thoughts and feelings about money. If you feel empty or lacking tell your Higher Self. Ask your Higher Self to help you feel full inside.

The Wholeness dimension is one we all strive to experience. During peak moments we know that we are whole and complete. That is when we ride waves of joy. We Dance. Go for that feeling as you write. Your Higher Self will guide you. Write as often and as much as you like. Shower your self with an abundance of love letters from your Higher Self.

–A Love Letter *to* My Higher Self–

Dear Higher Self,

_____

_____

_____

_____

_____

_____

_____

_____

_____

_____

_____

_____

_____

_____

_____

_____

_____

_____

_____

_____

_____

_____

_____

_____

_____

_____

_____

_____

_____

_____

_____

_____

_____

_____

_____

_____

_____

_____

_____

_____

_____

_____

_____

_____

_____

_____

_____

_____

_____

_____

(Your Signature)

Part II / NINE DIMENSIONS OF LOVE - 107

–A Love Letter *from* My Higher Self–

Dear _____   *(your name here),*

_____

_____

_____

_____

_____

_____

_____

_____

_____

_____

_____

_____

_____

_____

_____

_____

_____

_____

_____

_____

_____

_____

_____

_____

_____

_____

_____

_____

_____

_____

_____

_____

_____

_____

_____

_____

_____

_____

_____

_____

_____

_____

_____

_____

_____

_____

_____

_____

(Your Signature)

–My Appreciations–

Dear Higher Self,

Thank you.

_____
_____
_____
_____
_____
_____
_____
_____
_____
_____
_____
_____
_____

With love,

_____
(Your Signature)

The "Essence" Dimension

— 9 —

**An Invitation to
Love as Your Higher Self Loves.**

You and I are essentially infinite choice-makers.
In every moment of our existence,
we are in that field of all possibilities
where we have access to an infinity of choices.
—DEEPAK CHOPRA

–An Invitation to Love as Your Higher Self Loves–
A Love Letter from Your Higher Self

Dear _____

We have one more love letter for you today. In this love letter, we invite you to love as we do and to know your real essence. We invite you to remember that we are one—connected to an expanding and fulfilling Universe. You are essentially the designer and creator of your experience. Your essence qualities are your inner resources.

We are clarity, creativity and joy. We are abundance, balance and freedom. We are love, peace and health. We are magnificence, power and wisdom. You are all of these essential qualities as well.

When you love as we do, you live awake to your essence. Your life becomes a "dance with the universe." Feel your spirit soar, as you choreograph your sacred artistry—the steps of your dance.

Essence radiates through your work and turns it into play. Essence radiates into your relationships, inspiring intimate communion. Essence radiates into your dreams, releasing ideas as yet unborn in the physical dimension. Essence continually births new land in front of you. Universal reservoirs of love stimulate your creative juices. Enjoy being a conscious creator.

In the Essence Dimension of Love, desires blossom and are fulfilled within you. Pay attention to your desires. They are the seeds of your future creations.

Become an empowered creator, living awake to the Essence Dimension of Love. This is where real joy lives. We want you to have a good time while you are here.

Love is our essence and it is your essence too. A loving creator loves nothing more than to craft more vehicles and venues for love to pour through.

Whether you use your hands, your voice, or a hammer and nails, we invite you to open the Essence Dimension of Love where your desires manifest easily before you.

Whether you create with a smile on your face, a sparkle in your eyes or by celebrating the magnificence you see in others—you create endless experiences of love when you live connected to your essence.

Today, we invite you to remember your Essence.

I Love as my Higher Self loves.

We invite you to Love as we love and to enjoy ongoing waves of inspiration, passion and exhilaration. Love flows through you—as you—into the life you choose to experience. You are free to choose your life creations.

With Love,
Your Higher Self

–Love as Your Higher Self Loves–
... Dance with the Universe

WE HAVE ARRIVED at the dimension of our Higher Self. I have few words to add here. We are—each and every one of us—Magnificent Spiritual Beings having this amazing physical experience.

As my Higher Self reveals more of my essence to me, my human life is transforming. Where I once experienced relentless suffering, I now have tools that help me return to peace and tranquility. Where I previously worried and struggled, I am learning to connect with wisdom and joy as viable alternatives.

The Essence Dimension of Love is beyond logic and reason. We can barely grasp our essence while cloaked in our physical body suits. We do not have to understand it all in this moment.

Evolution is waking us up. Veils of forgetfulness are lifting. The love that is the essence of our Higher Self will not be kept out of our awareness much longer. It takes far more effort now to resist the essential goodness of life than to open up and say yes to it.

Yet, we do resist. We deny, hide and turn away from our brilliance. Together, we can lift the taboo on being brilliant. Every one of us is a creative genius. It is time we recognized and acknowledged our essence qualities.

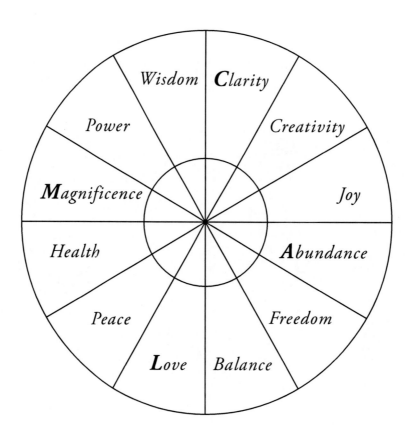

An Essence Mediation
Awaken Love as Your Higher Self

I am clarity, creativity and joy.
I am abundance, balance and freedom.
I am love, peace and health.
I am magnificence, power and wisdom.
All that my Higher Self is, I am also.

Explore The "Essence" Dimension
In Your Love Letters Writing Practice

Now it is time to connect with your essence qualities. Each of these qualities of spirit belong to you. They will empower the dance of your life. Explore each one of them. You might be surprised at the gifts they deliver you.

Write a Love Letter to your Higher Self exploring your thoughts and feelings about your:

- Clarity
- Creativity
- Joy

- Abundance
- Balance
- Freedom

- Love
- Peace
- Health

- Magnificence
- Power
- Wisdom

Ask your Higher Self to guide you to embrace each essence quality. Enjoy the process. Enjoy the Dance of your Life. Wherever you find yourself today is a great starting place. Expand from here. Use your Love Letters writing practice to know yourself, to connect with yourself, to express yourself and to rest in the wonder of your own Magnificence. Remember and celebrate who you really are.

—A Love Letter *to* My Higher Self—

Dear Higher Self,

_____

_____

_____

_____

_____

_____

_____

_____

_____

_____

_____

_____

_____

_____

_____

_____

_____

_____

_____

_____

_____

_____

_____

_____

_____

_____

_____

_____

_____

_____

_____

_____

_____

_____

_____

_____

_____

_____

_____

_____

_____

_____

_____

_____

_____

_____

_____

_____

_____

_____

_____

_____

_____

(Your Signature)

–A Love Letter *from* My Higher Self–

Dear _____   *(your name here),*

_____

_____

_____

_____

_____

_____

_____

_____

_____

_____

_____

_____

_____

_____

_____

_____

_____

_____

_____

_____

_____

_____

_____

_____

_____

_____

(Your Signature)

–My Appreciations–

Dear Higher Self,

    Thank you.

_____

_____

_____

_____

_____

_____

_____

_____

_____

_____

_____

_____

With love,

_____

(Your Signature)

−A Love Letter Post Script from Your Higher Self−

P.S. Regular Love Letter Writing Practice empowers you with insight and energy. It also gives us a place to communicate directly to you and with you. Please continue your Love Letter Writing Practice and let's not stop there.

We invite you to live the nine dimensions of love in your daily activities. We are with you celebrating you and helping you create the life experiences you choose. Enjoy the adventure. You intended to have a good time while you are here. We dance with you.

–Living the Nine Dimensions of Love–

Be fully *present*.

Accept your physicality and life

energy completely.

Focus for *connection* and

expression

guided by *intuition*.

Walk the Earth in *wholeness*,

consciously creating your life

from *essence*.

–Living the Nine Dimensions of Love–

The "Presence" Dimension	I love in current time and know that in this moment—right now—all is well and all is love.
The "Acceptance" Dimension	I love and accept my body and my sensations.
The "Energy" Dimension	I love all of my feelings and I let them be.
The "Focus" Dimension	I love my thoughts and focus them in loving ways.
The "Connection" Dimension	I love the entire cast of characters in my life and know that we are connected in love.
The "Expression" Dimension	I love my unique expressions
The "Intuition" Dimension	I love my expanding visions and trust my intuitions.
The "Wholeness" Dimension	I love my money. I am whole and full.
The "Essence" Dimension	I Love as my Higher Self loves.

Epilogue

EVOLVING THE HUMAN ENERGY SYSTEM

During this time of great awakening, we are collectively undergoing an evolutionary growth spurt. For those interested in the Chakras and how love awakens within our human energy systems, I include these extra notes.

The Nine Dimensions of Love outlined in this workbook parallel the spiritual centers in our individual energy systems. Each dimension radiates and expands from a specific chakra or energy center. As we evolve and grow to embody more and more of the love that we are, these energy centers fill with light, become more radiant and expand. We are changing from the inside out. As love infuses our consciousness, the manifest expression of this current transformation in our human form is only beginning to be known.

For healing practitioners, knowledge of the energy centers and the Nine Dimensions of Love, empowers us to understand our clients with greater clarity. We more easily invite them into their own Magnificence and fulfillment. As we each, in our own personal way, choose to awaken love through these nine dimensions, we inspire others to do so as well. We release our resistance to change, entertain positive possibilities and grow more capable of demonstrating the essential qualities of our Higher Selves.

Here then are the Nine Dimensions of Love as they awaken through our Chakras—or Spiritual Centers of Light within our Human Energy Systems.

–The "Presence" Dimension–

A choice to Love in Current Time opens our Grounding Point—an energy center approximately twelve inches below the feet. The Grounding Point provides an anchor for us to live as spiritual beings, consciously attracting and manifesting our desires into physical form.

–The "Acceptance" Dimension–

A CHOICE TO LOVE our Sensations and Bodies opens the Root Chakra—at the base of the spine. Here, we release inner conflicts, stop our fight with the physical world and relax into our eternal nature, while enjoying our physical experience.

–The "Energy" Dimension–

A CHOICE TO LOVE our Feelings opens the Belly Chakra—an energy center that includes our sexuality, and primal creative powers. Here, we embrace pleasure, light up with instinctive knowledge and feel energized from inside.

–The "Focus" Dimension–

A CHOICE TO LOVE our Thoughts opens the Solar Plexus—at the center of the torso. Here, we are empowered to take actions in alignment with our purpose and intention for our life.

–The "Connection" Dimension–

A CHOICE TO LOVE the Casts of Characters in our Lives opens the chakra—at the heart. Here, we transcend our tendency to blame and project onto others. Instead, we connect by taking full responsibility for our own happiness and fulfillment.

–The "Expression" Dimension–

A CHOICE TO LOVE our Uniqueness opens the creative energy center—within the throat. Here, our gifts, talents and offerings flourish and blossom. We offer our unique light to inspire others.

–The "Intuition" Dimension–

A CHOICE TO OPEN inner visions and to listen to our intuitions activates the energy center of the third eye. Here, our desires are fine-tuned, our self-knowledge expands and we embrace the evolution and expansion of our consciousness.

–The "Wholeness" Dimension–

A CHOICE TO LOVE our Fullness opens the Crown Chakra—at the top of the head. Here, we know we are whole, complete and full. We lack nothing and attract a steady flow of abundant resources and desired experiences.

–The "Essence" Dimension–

A CHOICE TO LOVE as our Higher Self Loves opens the Contact Point—approximately twelve inches above our head. Here, we know love, we are love, we express love and we see love everywhere in everything. Illusions of separation dissolve and our ongoing evolution becomes an exhilarating awakening to unity and oneness.

THIS IS A MAGNIFICENT TIME to be alive in physical form, to embody our Higher Self consciously and to radiate essence into the world. This beautiful evolutionary journey continues when we are awake and while we sleep.

Life is grand and love is everywhere. Please, love your evolution. Enjoy the adventure and Dance with the Universe. You are so very loved.

CELEBRATING COMPLETION

A Note of Appreciation from Peri

TODAY I FINISHED WRITING *Dancing with the Universe—Nine Dimensions of Love*. It is late in the day, in mid-October, on the very same day that racers are running the Ironman Triathalon here in Kona Hawaii.

For months now, I've been telling my friends that I feel I am turning the corner onto Alii Drive for the final lap of that grueling race. In years past, I have gone to the finish line to encourage late night racers, staggering toward their destination in darkness. We choose our own races, and while I have not chosen the path of a physical athlete, I admire and appreciate the energy of endurance that is in the air. It is no accident that I complete the writing of this workbook today.

Many people cheered me on and offered encouragement, as I stayed glued to my computer for long hours to get these words onto paper. Massage, acupuncture and long conversations with caring friends around the globe helped me maintain stamina. Love from a variety of sources carried me.

Now, I imagine walks along the beach, returning to dance and yoga classes and – I must admit – more writing. I just love the process and I don't intend to stop here. The next books are already kicking inside of me. But, I'll take a rest first – for replenishment, for my own Dance with the Universe and to live the Nine Dimensions of Love. I so appreciate this ride.

About the Author

FOR MORE THAN TWENTY YEARS Peri Coeurtney Enkin has inspired individuals, couples and group to live their deep-heart dreams and experience freedom, peace and fulfillment. People around the world find their lives enriched by her combination of practical down-to-earth skills and heart–centered processes for spiritual awakening.

Peri is the founder of Creators Choice and the author of *Love Letters from Your Higher Self* and *Dancing with the Universe; Nine Dimensions of Love.* She has created countless life enhancement programs, including the Love Letters Path for Personal Growth, The Core Training, The Turnaround, Dancing with the Universe, Aware Entrepreneurs, and Whole Person.

Peri lives in beautiful Hawaii, and welcomes you to experience the essence of Aloha in her writing and her teachings.

Resources

Download additional love letter writing practice worksheets here:

http://www.creatorschoice.com/resources

Please visit our website to share your comments
and to learn about additional resources.

www.CreatorsChoice.com

CPSIA information can be obtained at www.ICGtesting.com
Printed in the USA
LVOW030930080212

267703LV00001B/19/P

9 780982 121313